Beloved daughter of the

Holy Prophet Muhammad

(May peace and blessings of Allah be upon him)

ḤAḌRAT ZAINAB

(May Allah be pleased with her)

Ḥaḍrat Zainab

(English rendering of an Urdu book Ḥaḍrat Zainab)

Rendered into English by: Children's Book Team of

Additional Wakālat-e-Taṣnīf

First published in English in the United Kingdom in 2014

Published by:

Additional Wakālat-e-Taṣnīf
(Islam International Publications Ltd.)
Islamabad, Sheephatch Lane
Tilford, Surrey GU10 2AQ, UK

Printed in the UK at:
Raqeem Press
Tilford, Surrey, GU10 2AQ

For more information please visit: www.alislam.org

ISBN: 978-1-84880-845-4

TABLE OF CONTENTS

Foreword......*i*
Map......*iii*
Family Tree......*v*
1 Eldest Daughter of Exalted Parents......7
2 Marriage......11
3 Acceptance of Islam......13
4 Persecution by the Makkans......17
5 A Precious Ransom......19
6 A Daughter's Difficult Migration......21
7 A Beautiful Marriage......25
8 A Generous and Honourable Man......29
9 The Love of Grandchildren......33
10 Martyrdom......37
Publisher's Note......41
Glossary......45
Study Guide and Workbook......47
References......61

In the name of Allah, the Gracious, the Merciful,
We praise Him and invoke His blessings upon His Noble Messenger

FOREWORD

These books were originally published in Urdu to provide children with a basic knowledge and understanding of revered figures from our religious history. Illustrations, children's activities and glossaries have been added to enhance the learning experience for children. The goal of these books is for children to develop a love and appreciation for the profound faith and the immense sacrifices of the revered personalities portrayed in these books. It is also hoped that the examples of righteousness found in these pages inspire children to cultivate a personal relationship with Allah, our Creator and Sustainer.

This particular book is about the life of Ḥaḍrat Zainab[ra], the daughter of our beloved Master, the Holy Prophet Muhammad[sa]. Some modifications and additions have been made to the original text for the sake of historical accuracy and style.

This book was rendered into English by the Children's Book Team of Additional Wakālat-e-Taṣnīf headed by Uzma Saeed Ahmad and Noma Saeed Samee, and includes: Busaina Ahmad, Hafia Khan, Rafia Rehana Khattak and Amina Maryem Shams. May Allah the Almighty reward them abundantly in this world and the hereafter. ***Amīn***.

Munir-ud-Din Shams
Additional Wakīlut-Taṣnīf
July 2014

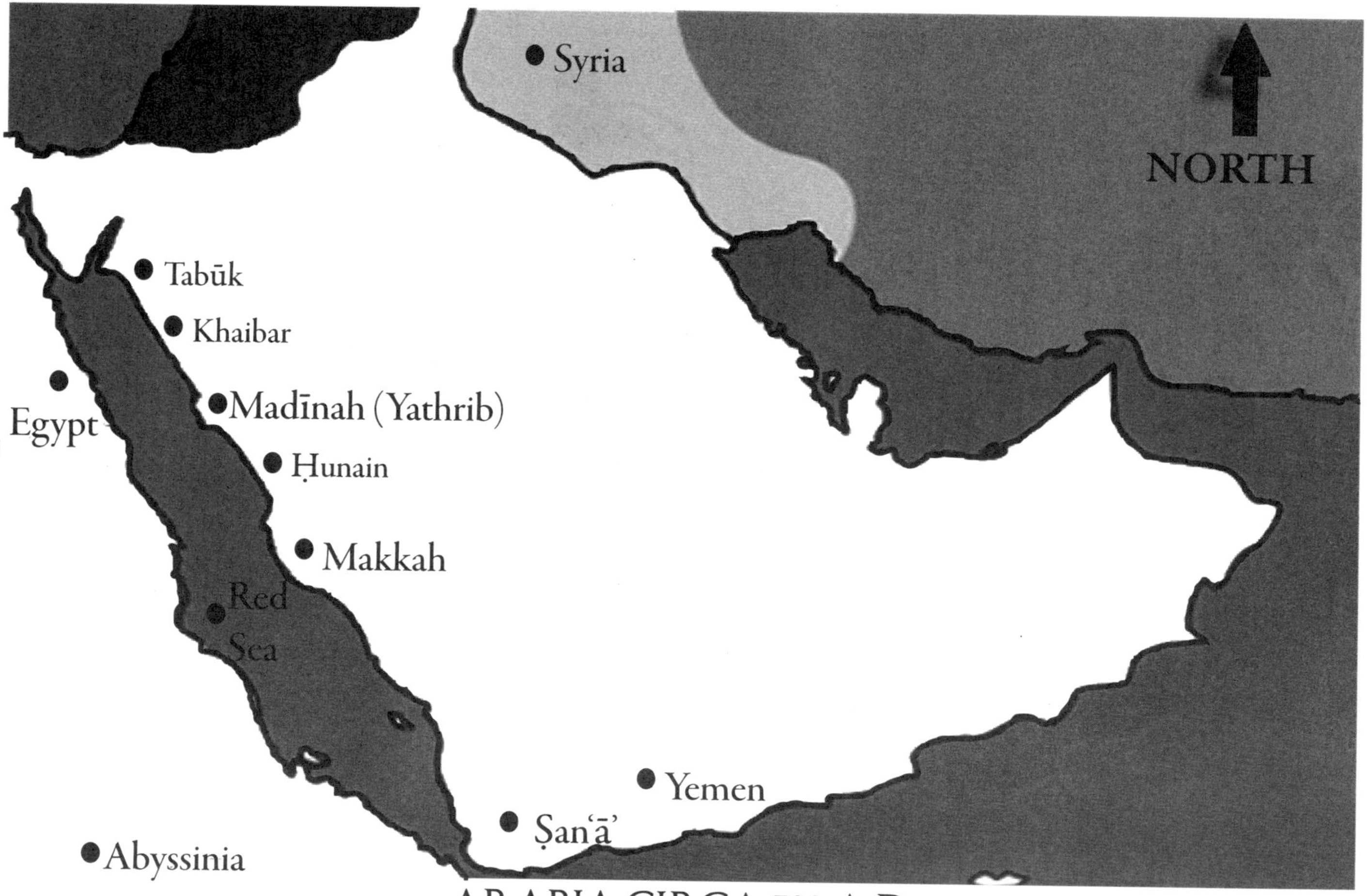

ARABIA CIRCA 700 A.D

FAMILY TREE OF ḤAḌRAT ZAINAB[RA]

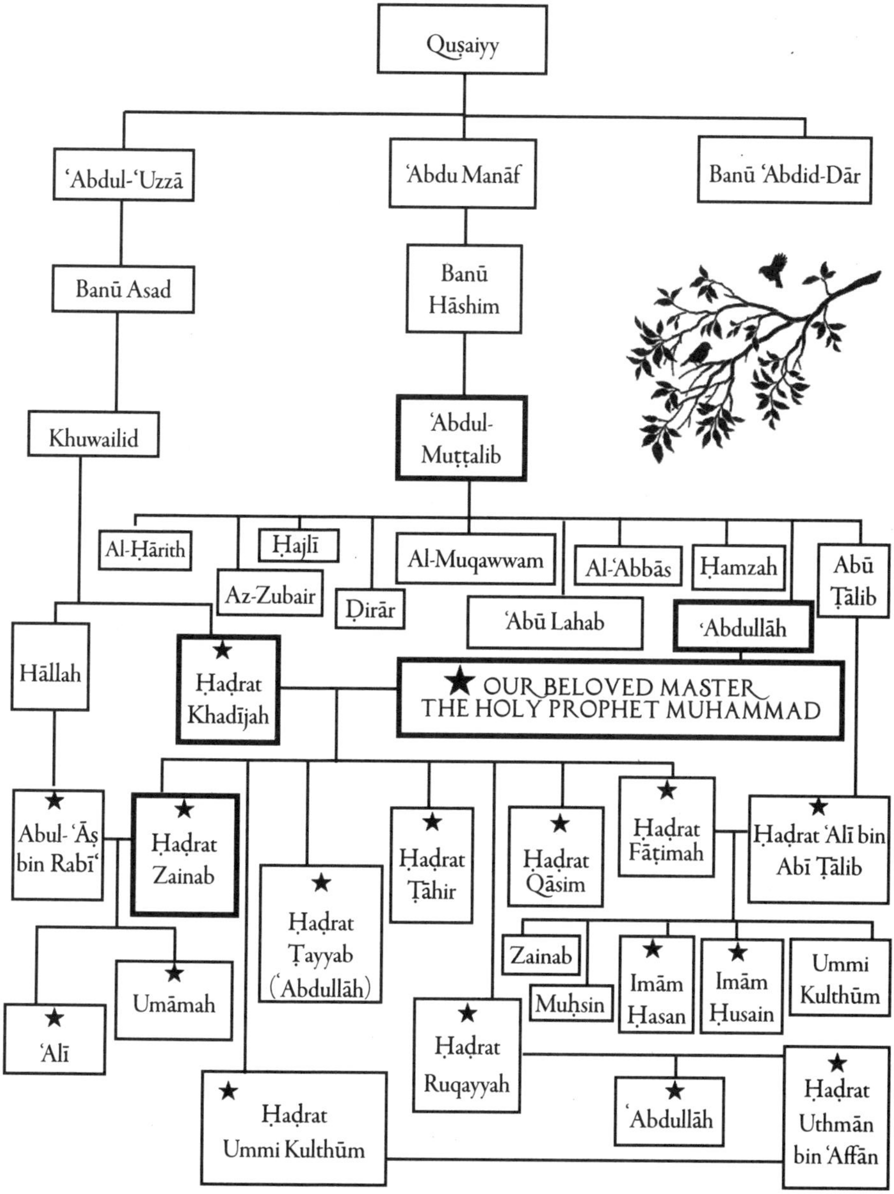
Quṣaiyy
'Abdul-'Uzzā
'Abdu Manāf
Banū 'Abdid-Dār
Banū Asad
Banū Hāshim
Khuwailid
'Abdul-Muṭṭalib
Al-Ḥārith
Ḥajlī
Az-Zubair
Ḍirār
Al-Muqawwam
'Abū Lahab
Al-'Abbās
Ḥamzah
'Abdullāh
Abū Ṭālib
Hāllah
Ḥaḍrat Khadījah
OUR BELOVED MASTER THE HOLY PROPHET MUHAMMAD
Abul- 'Āṣ bin Rabī'
Ḥaḍrat Zainab
Ḥaḍrat Ṭayyab ('Abdullāh)
Ḥaḍrat Ṭāhir
Ḥaḍrat Qāsim
Ḥaḍrat Fāṭimah
Ḥaḍrat 'Alī bin Abī Ṭālib
Umāmah
'Alī
Zainab
Muḥsin
Imām Ḥasan
Imām Ḥusain
Ummi Kulthūm
Ḥaḍrat Ruqayyah
Ḥaḍrat Ummi Kulthūm
'Abdullāh
Ḥaḍrat Uthmān bin 'Affān

1
ELDEST DAUGHTER OF EXALTED PARENTS

Ḥaḍrat Zainab[ra] was the eldest daughter of our beloved Master, the Holy Prophet Muhammad[sa] and his first wife, Ḥaḍrat Khadījah[ra]. She was the daughter of the most exalted parents in the entire history of the world. Before the advent of the Holy Prophet[sa] people in Arabia used to bury their daughters alive. Even if the girls were allowed to live, they were not given any love or affection. They were not given any rights as human beings and were treated like animals. Allah sent the Holy Prophet[sa] as a mercy for the whole world. The Holy Prophet[sa] came and established great honour and respect for women. He taught people that daughters should be cherished. In fact, he said that anyone who raises two or more daughters with love and kindness would be as close to him in paradise as his two fingers are close to each other.

Ḥaḍrat Zainab[ra] was born several years before the prophethood of the Holy Prophet[sa]. The age of the Holy Prophet[sa] was thirty years at the time of her birth. Her family tree from her exalted father's side was like this; Ḥaḍrat Zainab[ra] was the daughter of Muhammad[sa], who was the son of 'Abdullāh, who was the son of 'Abdul-Muṭṭalib, who was the son of Hāshim, who was the son of Manāf, who was the son of Quṣaiyy. Her family tree from the side of her honoured mother, Ḥaḍrat Khadījah[ra] was like this; Ḥaḍrat Zainab[ra] was the daughter of Ḥaḍrat Khadījah[ra], who was the daughter of Khuwailid, who was the son of Asad, who was the son of 'Abdul-'Uzzā, who was the son of Quṣaiyy.[1]

Her mother Ḥaḍrat Khadījah[ra] educated Ḥaḍrat Zainab[ra] with a lot of care. Ḥaḍrat Khadījah[ra] was a highly intelligent, well-mannered, and refined lady. She was a very beloved and caring wife of the Holy Prophet[sa]. Ḥaḍrat Khadījah[ra] stood shoulder to shoulder with the Holy Prophet[sa] in all his sorrows and difficulties. As the beloved first-born child Ḥaḍrat Zainab[ra] received a lot of love and inherited a wealth of noble traits from her parents.

2
MARRIAGE

The wedding of Ḥaḍrat Zainab[ra] took place before the prophethood of her father, the Holy Prophet[sa]. According to the custom of the Arabs, she was married at an early age to her cousin Ḥaḍrat Abul-'Āṣ[ra] bin Rabī'. Ḥaḍrat Abul-'Āṣ[ra] was the son of Hāllah. Hāllah was the sister of Ḥaḍrat Khadījah[ra] and daughter of Khuwailid.

At the occasion of her eldest daughter's wedding Ḥaḍrat Khadījah[ra] gave her a beautiful gift, a garnet necklace made in Yemen. This was the finest piece of jewelry Ḥaḍrat Khadījah[ra] owned and she wanted to give it to her daughter as a part of her dowry.

3
ACCEPTANCE OF ISLAM

When the Holy Prophet[sa] made the claim of prophethood, Ḥaḍrat Zainab[ra] immediately accepted Islam. At that time her husband was on a business trip away from Makkah. During his travel Ḥaḍrat Abul-'Āṣ[ra] heard reports about the claim of the Holy Prophet[sa]. This news was confirmed upon his return to Makkah when Ḥaḍrat Zainab[ra] told him that she had accepted Islam.

Ḥaḍrat Abul-'Āṣ[ra] was bewildered by this information and asked, "O Zainab, did you not even think about what would happen if I did not accept the claim of the Holy Prophet[sa]?"

Ḥaḍrat Zainab[ra] replied, "How can I reject my father who is ***Ṣādiq*** (Truthful) and ***Amīn*** (Trustworthy)? I swear by God, he is telling the truth. My mother and sisters, Ḥaḍrat 'Alī[ra] son of Abū Ṭālib, Abū Bakr[ra], Ḥaḍrat 'Uthmān[ra] bin 'Affān from your tribe, and your cousin Ḥaḍrat Zubair[ra] bin Al-'Awwām have all accepted Islam. I do not think that you will reject my father's claim of prophethood."

Ḥaḍrat Abul-'Āṣ[ra] said, "I have no doubt about your father nor do I reject him. Indeed, nothing is more important to me than to be with you in your religion, but I am afraid that my people will accuse me of abandoning the religion of my ancestors for my wife's sake." Therefore he did not accept Islam[2]. However, he was an honourable and affectionate person. The Holy Prophet[sa] often expressed appreciation for the excellent relationship between him and Ḥaḍrat Zainab[ra].

Ḥaḍrat Abul-‘Āṣ[ra] was travelling with a caravan when he learned that Ḥaḍrat Zainab[ra] had accepted Islam.

4
PERSECUTION BY THE MAKKANS

As Islam achieved greater success in Makkah the hostility to it also kept rising. The disbelievers did not let any opportunity pass in which they could inflict hardship on the Holy Prophet[sa]. Sometimes they gave the Holy Prophet[sa] physical hardship and on other occasions, they caused him emotional suffering.

Two of the daughters of the Holy Prophet[sa], Ḥaḍrat Ruqayyah[ra] and Ḥaḍrat Ummi Kulthūm[ra], were engaged to marry two of Abū Lahab's sons. After the Holy Prophet [sa] claimed to be a prophet of God, both of them broke their ties with the daughters of the Holy Prophet[sa], according to the wishes of Abū Lahab.[3] Some of the leaders of the Quraish tried to force Ḥaḍrat Abul-'Āṣ[ra] to divorce Ḥaḍrat Zainab[ra] as well. As an encouragement they offered to marry Ḥaḍrat Abul-'Āṣ[ra] to a girl from another honourable tribe of the Quraish. Their goal was to cause emotional pain to the Holy Prophet[sa].

However, Ḥaḍrat Abul-'Āṣ[ra] loved Ḥaḍrat Zainab[ra] very much and he completely rejected this evil offer of the Makkans. Although he had still not changed his religion at the time of the migration of the Holy Prophet[sa] to Madīnah, the Holy Prophet[sa] liked him and praised him highly.[4]

In the thirteenth year of his advent, the Holy Prophet[sa] migrated from Makkah to the city of Madīnah. During this period Ḥaḍrat Zainab[ra] was living with her in-laws. Soon after the migration, the first battle of Islam was fought between the Muslims and disbelievers of Makkah. This battle was called the Battle of Badr. Ḥaḍrat Abul-'Āṣ[ra] fought on the side of the Makkans against the Muslims.[5]

5

A PRECIOUS RANSOM

Ḥaḍrat Zainab[ra] was still living in Makkah at this time. At the Battle of Badr the Muslims defeated the Makkans and some of the disbelievers were held as captives. Ḥaḍrat Abul-'Āṣ[ra] was among those taken captive.

When the news of their captivity reached Makkah the relatives of the captives sent ransom to gain their release. Ḥaḍrat Zainab[ra] gave her brother-in-law the garnet necklace that was a wedding gift from her mother. She offered her valuable necklace to be used as ransom to gain freedom for Ḥaḍrat Abul-'Āṣ[ra].

When the Holy Prophet[sa] saw the necklace among the

articles of ransom his eyes welled up. It reminded him of his beloved wife, Ḥaḍrat Khadījah[ra], who had passed away after the cruel boycott which forced the Muslims to take refuge in the valley of Abī Ṭālib. The memories of his wife came back to him at the sight of the necklace. The Holy Prophet[sa] asked the Muslims if they would set Ḥaḍrat Abul-ʿĀṣ[ra] free and return the necklace as well. This is because the necklace was very precious and dear to the Holy Prophet[sa] and reminded him of his beloved wife Ḥaḍrat Khadījah[ra]. The companions immediately fulfilled this wish of the Holy Prophet[sa] with complete sincerity, love, and obedience. Therefore Ḥaḍrat Abul-ʿĀṣ[ra] was set free and the necklace was returned to Ḥaḍrat Zainab[ra].

6
A DAUGHTER'S DIFFICULT MIGRATION

All the Makkan prisoners were released with the payment of a ransom. It was against the dignity of prophethood that the son-in-law of the Holy Prophet[sa] should be released without paying any ransom. Therefore, it was decided that after returning to Makkah Ḥaḍrat Abul-'Āṣ[ra] would send Ḥaḍrat Zainab[ra] to Madīnah as payment for his ransom.[6]

The Holy Prophet[sa] instructed Ḥaḍrat Abul-'Āṣ[ra] and Ḥaḍrat Zaid[ra] bin Ḥārithah, the adopted son of the Holy Prophet[sa], to bring Ḥaḍrat Zainab[ra] to Madīnah. Ḥaḍrat Zaid[ra] was instructed to stay outside of Makkah and wait for Ḥaḍrat Zainab[ra], then bring her back to

Madīnah. Ḥaḍrat Abul-'Āṣ[ra] instructed his younger brother to accompany Ḥaḍrat Zainab[ra] on her journey from Makkah.

When preparations for the journey were complete, Ḥaḍrat Zainab[ra] mounted her camel and departed for Madīnah. Her brother-in-law Kinānah bin Rabī' accompanied her. As it was expected that the disbelievers of Makkah would cause trouble, her brother-in-law was armed with arrows and a bow.

When the disbelievers learned that Ḥaḍrat Zainab[ra] had left Makkah, they became extremely angry. The people of Makkah chased after them and surrounded them at a place called Dhī Ṭuwā outside of Makkah. A person named Habbār bin Aswad and another man from this group attacked Ḥaḍrat Zainab[ra] with a spear. Ḥaḍrat Zainab[ra] fell from the camel to the ground. As a result of this attack she suffered a terrible wound deep inside of her stomach. She lost a great deal of blood from this injury.

Her brother-in-law took an arrow out of his quiver and warned the disbelievers that if anyone came near them he would shoot them with his arrow. At this threat the disbelievers quickly dispersed. Abū Sufyān, the leader of the Quraish came forward and said that he wanted to talk. Kinānah put his arrow back in its quiver and asked what he wanted to discuss. Abū Sufyan said we have suffered a humiliating defeat, misfortune, and disgrace at the hands of Muhammad[sa]. If you take the daughter of Muhammad[sa] from among us, we will be considered weak and cowards. We have no reason to prevent the daughter of Muhammad[sa] from leaving Makkah if she so wishes. However, my goal is that you return to Makkah for now and when the situation settles down you can take her to Madīnah.

Kinānah agreed to this and after a few days he discreetly handed her over to Ḥaḍrat Zaid[ra] bin Ḥārithah who brought her back from Makkah.[7]

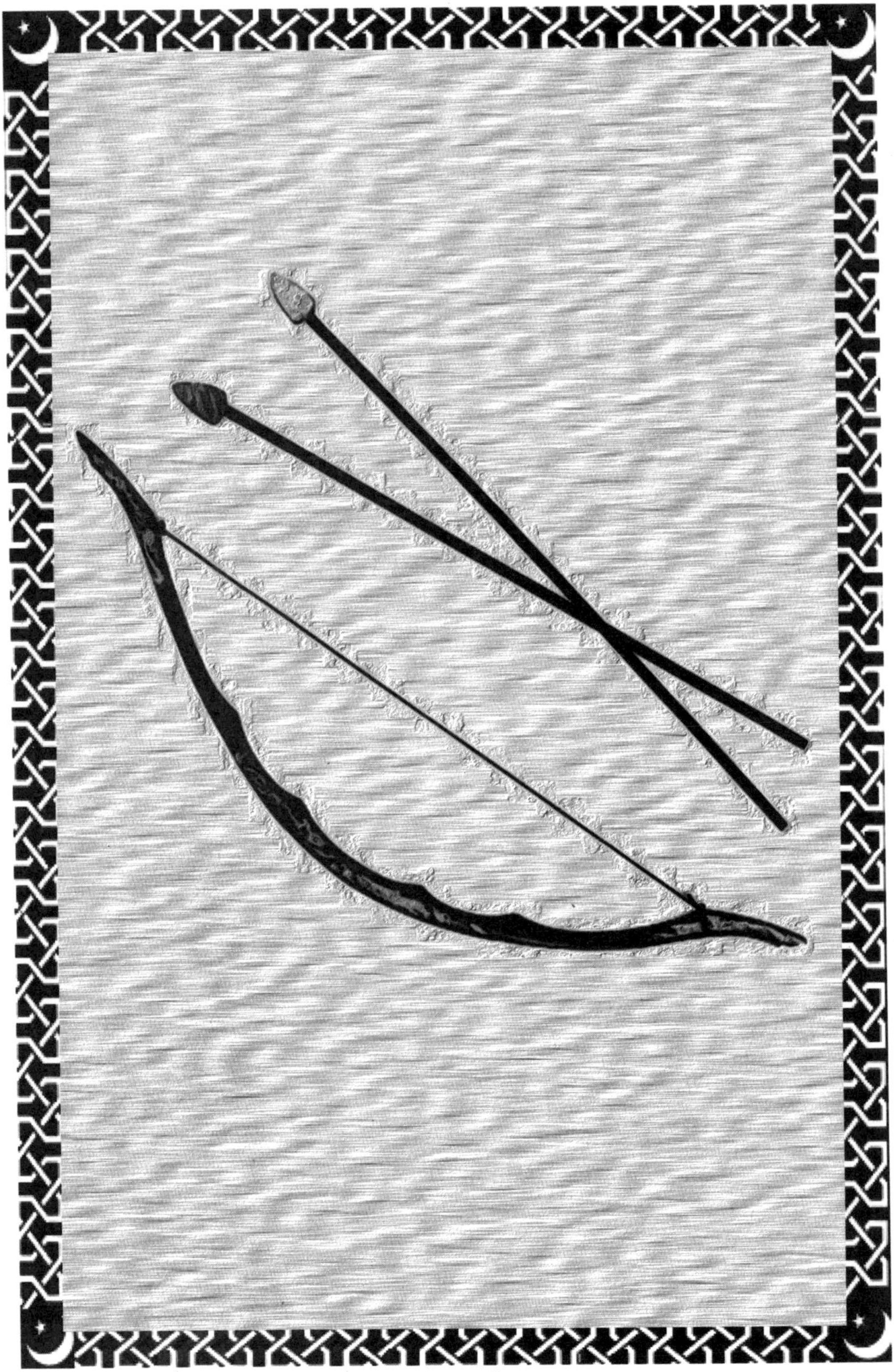

An ancient Arabian bow and arrow

7
A BEAUTIFUL MARRIAGE

Ḥaḍrat Zainab[ra] was injured so severely that she lived only a few years after being wounded. For the rest of her life she suffered great agony due to the severity of her wound.

The knowledge of her ill health grieved the Holy Prophet[sa] deeply and he once said, "She was my best daughter and she was tried due to her love for me."

The departure of Ḥaḍrat Zainab[ra] to Madīnah grieved Ḥaḍrat Abul-'Āṣ[ra] greatly because they had a beautiful relationship full of love and affection. Any separation from her made him very sorrowful. Once while on a journey to Syria he remembered Ḥaḍrat

Zainab[ra] with these words full of anguish, "When I went past Iram and I remembered Zainab, a prayer for her naturally came to me that, 'O Allah! Keep her strong and healthy, she who is residing at a sacred place (Makkah); she who is the daughter of the Trustworthy (Muhammad[sa]); give her the best reward. Surely, a husband praises that which he knows well." Both husband and wife had to suffer six difficult years of separation.[7B]

Ḥaḍrat Abul-'Āṣ[ra] was highly honest and a successful merchant. Once it so happened that he was returning from a business trip to Syria with a caravan of the Quraish. When the Holy Prophet[sa] learned about this caravan he sent Ḥaḍrat Zaid[ra] bin Ḥārithah with one hundred and seventy riders to follow it. The Muslims apprehended the disbelievers at the place of 'Īṣ. Since the Muslims recognized Ḥaḍrat Abul-'Āṣ[ra], he was not stopped. When Ḥaḍrat Abul-'Āṣ[ra] saw the plight of the caravan he immediately went to Madīnah and asked the protection of Ḥaḍrat Zainab[ra]. It was a custom among the Arabs that if one person extended protection to someone the whole tribe was bound by it.

At the time the Holy Prophet[sa] was offering Fajr

Prayer. Ḥaḍrat Zainab[ra] called out that she had taken Ḥaḍrat Abul-'Āṣ[ra] under her protection. After completing his prayer the Holy Prophet[sa] asked, "O people! Did you hear anything?" They replied saying, "Yes!"

When the Holy Prophet[sa] came home Ḥaḍrat Zainab[ra] came to see him and said, "O Prophet of Allah! From the closer of relations Abul-'Āṣ[ra] is my first cousin and a more distant relation he is the father of my children. This is why I have extended protection to him.[8] Abul-'Āṣ[ra] was the leader of this caravan therefore please kindly return their possessions."

The Holy Prophet[sa] addressed the people saying "You know Abul-'Āṣ[ra] is my relative. If you choose to favour him by returning his possessions it will make me happy. However, you have the authority to do as you wish." All the people agreed to return everything.

FAJR
PRAYER IS
BETTER THAN
SLEEP

8

A GENEROUS AND HONOURABLE MAN

The Holy Prophet[sa] instructed Ḥaḍrat Zainab[ra] to take good care of Abul-'Āṣ[ra] and to treat him with respect. However, he instructed that they should live in separate houses until Ḥaḍrat Abul-'Āṣ[ra] accepted Islam. After that Ḥaḍrat Abul-'Āṣ[ra] took his possessions, kissed his children, bid farewell to his wife and left.[9]

Upon his return to Makkah Ḥaḍrat Abul-'Āṣ[ra] cleared all his accounts and one day gathered the Quraish together and asked them if anyone had any claim on him. They replied, "Indeed, now we have no claim concerning you. May God reward you in an excellent manner. You are indeed an honourable and generous person."

At this moment Ḥaḍrat Abul-'Āṣ[ra] declared that he had become a Muslim, and openly recited the ***Kalimah***. He swore by God that the only thing that had kept him from the companionship of the Holy Prophet[sa] was that the people might think he had accepted Islam in order to be freed from any monetary obligations. Now that he had fully discharged all his obligations, nothing could keep him from becoming a Muslim.

This incidence shows the greatness of his character. Ḥaḍrat Abul-'Āṣ[ra] was the son-in-law of the most trustworthy person in the world, the Holy Prophet[sa] and he was exemplary in his loyalty to that relationship.

In the seventh year after the ***Hijrah***, during the month of Muḥarram, Ḥaḍrat Abul-'Āṣ[ra] accepted Islam and migrated from Makkah to Madīnah. After his arrival in Madīnah the Holy Prophet[sa] sent Ḥaḍrat Zainab[ra] to live with him.[10]

There is none worthy of worship except Allah,
Muhammad is the Messenger of Allah.

9
THE LOVE OF GRANDCHILDREN

Ḥaḍrat Zainab[ra] loved her illustrious father and her husband, Abul-ʿĀṣ[ra], very much. She used to wear very nice clothes. The attendant of the Holy Prophet[sa], Ḥaḍrat Anas[ra] once saw her wearing a beautiful yellow-striped silk shawl.

Ḥaḍrat Zainab[ra] had two children. Her son's name was ʿAlī[ra] and her daughter's name was Umāmah[ra]. ʿAlī[ra] was born in Makkah before the migration. He was very dear to the Holy Prophet[sa]. The Holy Prophet[sa] had trained him personally. After the conquest of Makkah he was riding on the camel with the Holy Prophet[sa] when the Holy Prophet[sa] entered Makkah. According to some traditions he was alive at the occasion of the Battle of Yarmūk which was fought during the ***Khilāfat*** of Ḥaḍrat 'Umar[ra]. According to some other accounts he passed away before reaching his maturity.

The Holy Prophet[sa] loved the daughter of Ḥaḍrat Zainab[ra], Ḥaḍrat Umāmah[ra], deeply. She was the first granddaughter of the Holy Prophet[sa]. Ḥaḍrat Umāmah[ra] was so dear to the Holy Prophet[sa] that he would not part with her even when offering prayers. He would seat her on his shoulders while offering prayer. When the Holy Prophet[sa] would move to his bowing position and prostration, he would lay her down. Then, when he would raise his head from prostration, he would seat her on his shoulders again. The Holy Prophet[sa] would follow this routine through the completion of his prayer. This incident shows the immense love that the Holy Prophet[sa] had for daughters.

Once the Holy Prophet[sa] received a precious necklace as a gift. The Holy Prophet[sa] came home and said that he would give it to the person who was most dear to him in the family. It was presumed that the Mother of the Believers, Ḥaḍrat 'Ā'ishah[ra], would receive it, but the Holy Prophet[sa] put the necklace around the neck of Ḥaḍrat Umāmah[ra].

After the demise of Ḥaḍrat Fāṭimah[ra], who was the maternal aunt of Ḥaḍrat Umāmah[ra], she was married to Ḥaḍrat 'Alī[ra] in fulfilment of the wish of Ḥaḍrat Fāṭimah[ra].[11]

10
MARTYRDOM

Ḥaḍrat Zainab[ra] lived a little over a year after Ḥaḍrat Abul-'Āṣ[ra] accepted Islam. The cause of her death was the same wound that she received at the time of her migration. This places her in the circle of martyrs. She passed away in the eighth year after the ***Hijrah***. The Holy Prophet[sa] pronounced a death sentence for Habbār bin Aswad who had inflicted the wound on her. However, he pardoned the murderer of his beloved daughter when he asked for forgiveness at the time of the conquest of Makkah.

اَللّٰھُمَّ صَلِّ عَلٰی مُحَمَّدٍ

Allahūmma ṣalli ʿalā Muḥammad

O Allah! Shower your blessings on Muhammad.

Ḥaḍrat ʿAṭiyyah[ra], Ḥaḍrat Ummi Aiman[ra], Ḥaḍrat Saudah[ra] and Ḥaḍrat Ummi Salamah[ra] washed the body of Ḥaḍrat Zainab.

The Holy Prophet[sa] was informed after the body of Ḥaḍrat Zainab[ra] had been washed. The Holy Prophet[sa] offered his own mantle to be placed on the body inside the shroud. The Holy Prophet[sa] also instructed that all parts of the body should be washed three or five times and camphor should be applied on the body. It is also narrated that the Holy Prophet[sa] said "O Ummi ʿAṭiyyah[ra]! Wrap my daughter in this shroud in the best manner, braid her hair in three parts, and apply the best perfumes on her."

The Holy Prophet[sa] himself led his daughter's funeral prayer, lowered her into the grave and she was buried in ***Jannatul-Baqīʿ***. The Holy Prophet[sa]'s grief was evident from his face. Recalling the suffering of Ḥaḍrat Zainab[ra] the Holy Prophet[sa] prayed, "O Allah! Ease the suffering of

Zainab[ra] and make the confined space of the grave spacious for her."

Ḥaḍrat Abul-'Āṣ[ra] was dejected and grief stricken at the demise of Ḥaḍrat Zainab[ra]. He also passed away shortly afterwards.

اِنَّـا لِلّٰهِ وَ اِنَّا اِلَيْهِ رٰجِعُوْنَ

innā lillāhi wa innā ilaihi rāji'ūn

To Allah we belong and to Him shall we return.

May God raise the ranks of these righteous and noble individuals and grant us the ability to follow in their footsteps. ***Āmīn.***

إِنَّا لِلَّٰهِ وَإِنَّا إِلَيْهِ رَاجِعُونَ

(Baqarah, Verse 157)

TO ALLAH WE BELONG AND
TO HIM SHALL WE RETURN

PUBLISHER'S NOTE

The following abbreviations have been used. Readers are urged to recite the full salutations when reading the book:

sa ***ṣallallāhu 'alaihi wa sallam***, meaning 'may peace and blessings of Allah be upon him,' is written after the name of the Holy Prophet Muhammad[sa].

as ***'alaihis-salām,*** meaning 'may peace be on him,' is written after the name of Prophets other than the Holy Prophet Muhammad[sa].

ra ***raḍiyallāhu 'anhu/'anhā/'anhum***, meaning 'may Allah be pleased with him/her/them,' is written after the names of the Companions of the Holy Prophet Muhammad[sa] or of the Promised Messiah[as].

In transliterating Arabic words we have adopted the following system established by the Royal Asiatic Society.

ا at the beginning of a word, pronounced as ***a, i, u*** preceded by a very slight aspiration, like *h* in the English word ***honour***.

ث ***th***, pronounced like *th* in the English word ***thing.***

ح ***ḥ***, a guttural aspirate, stronger than ***h***.

خ ***kh***, pronounced like the Scotch *ch* in ***loch***.

ذ ***dh***, pronounced like the English *th* in ***that***.

ص *ṣ*, strongly articulated *s*.

ض *ḍ*, similar to the English *th* in *this*.

ط *ṭ*, strongly articulated palatal *t*.

ظ *ẓ*, strongly articulated *z*.

ع ‘, a strong guttural, the pronunciation of which must be learnt by the ear.

غ *gh*, a sound approached very nearly in the *r grasseye* in French, and in the German *r*. It requires the muscles of the throat to be in the 'gargling' position whilst pronouncing it.

ق *q*, a deep guttural *k* sound.

ء ’, a sort of catch in the voice.

Short vowels are represented by:

a for —َ— (like *u* in *bud*)

i for —ِ— (like *i* in *bid*)

u for —ُ— (like *oo* in *wood*)

Long vowels by:

ā for —ا— or آ (like *a* in *father*);

ī for ی—ِ— or —ٖ— (like *ee* in *deep*);

ū for و—ُ— (like *oo* in *root*);

Other:

ai for ی—َ— (like *i* in *site*);

au for و ـَـ (resembling *ou* in *sound*)

The consonants not included in the above list have the same phonetic value as in the principal languages of Europe. While the Arabic ن is represented by ***n***, we have indicated the Urdu ں as ***ń***. Curved commas are used in the system of transliteration, ‘ for ع , ’ for ء.

We have not transliterated certain Arabic words which have become part of English language. The Royal Asiatic Society rules of transliteration for names of persons, places and other terms, could not be followed throughout the book as many of the names contain non-Arabic characters and carry a local transliteration and pronunciation style which in itself is also not consistent either.

The Publisher

GLOSSARY

Allah— Allah is the personal name of God in Islam. To show proper reverence to Him, Muslims often add Ta'ālā, 'the Most High,' when saying His Holy name.

Ḥadīth— A saying of the Holy Prophet Muhammad[sa]. The plural is aḥādīth.

Ḥaḍrat — A term of respect used for a person of established righteousness and piety.

Hijrah— Year of Islamic calendar that started after the migration of the Holy Prophet[sa].

Holy Prophet[sa] — A term used exclusively for Ḥaḍrat Muhammad[sa], the Prophet of Islam.

Islam— Means peace and submission; Name of religion brought by the Holy Prophet Muhammad[sa].

Jannatul-Baqī'— Graveyard in Madīnah where many Companions of the Holy Prophet[sa] are buried

Kalimah Ṭayyibah— The creed of Islam, There is none worthy of worship except Allah, and Muhammad[sa] is the Messenger of Allah.

Khilāfat— Divine system of succession after the prophet.

Makkah—City of the birth of the Holy Prophet[sa] and location of the Ka'bah.

Madīnah— City to which the Holy Prophet[sa] migrated. Its former name was Yathrib.

Quraish— the most highly respected tribe in Arabia.

Ummahātul-Mu'minīn[ra]—Mothers of all Believers. Title given to all the wives of the Holy Prophet[sa]. This title is based on the words of Allah the Almighty Who refers to them as 'Mothers' in the Holy Quran. (Singular is Ummul-Mu'minīn - Mother of the Believers)

Beloved daughter of the Holy Prophet Muhammad[sa]

ḤAḌRAT ZAINAB

(May Allah be pleased with her)

STUDY GUIDE AND WORKBOOK

THE WORDS OF OUR BELOVED PROPHET[SA]

FROM THE BOOKS OF ḤADĪTH MUSLIM AND TIRMIDHĪ

"Whoever raises two girls until they reach maturity and get married, he and I will be like these two on the Day of Resurrection" and the Holy Prophet[sa] held together two of his fingers. (Narrated by Muslim and At-Tirmidhī.)

Explain what you think this Hadīth means.________________________

____

____

____

Give an example from the book which shows how much the Holy Prophet[sa] loved his daughters. ________________________

____

____

____

____

Can you think of or find any other Aḥādīth which show the high regard that the Holy Prophet[sa] had for women and daughters? Write it and explain what it means.________________________

____

____

____

____

____

____

WHO SAID IT?

Using the key below, draw the picture that represents the person who said the quote.

Holy Prophet Muhammad[sa]

Ḥaḍrat Zainab[ra]

Ḥaḍrat Abul-'Āṣ[ra]

The Quraish

QUOTE: **SYMBOL:**

"How can I reject my father who is ***Ṣādiq*** (Truthful) and ***Amīn*** (Trustworthy)? I swear by God, he is telling the truth. My mother and sisters, Ḥaḍrat 'Alī[ra] son of Abū Ṭālib, Abū Bakr[ra], Ḥaḍrat 'Uthmān[ra] bin 'Affān from your tribe, and your cousin Ḥaḍrat Zubair[ra] bin Al-'Awwām have all accepted Islam. I do not think that you will reject my father's claim of prophethood."

"Indeed now we have no claim concerning you, may God reward you in excellent manner, you are indeed an honourable and generous person".

QUOTE:	SYMBOL:
"O Allah! Ease the suffering of Ḥaḍrat Zainab[ra] and make the confined space of the grave spacious for her."	
"I have no doubt about your father nor do I reject him. Indeed, nothing is more important to me than to be with you in your religion, but I am afraid that my people will accuse me of abandoning the religion of my ancestors for my wife's sake."	
"O Ummi 'Aṭiyyah[ra]! Wrap my daughter in the shroud in the best manner, braid her hair in three parts, and apply the best perfumes on her."	
"O Prophet of Allah! From the closer relation Abul-'Āṣ[ra] is my first cousin and from a more distant relation he is the father of my children. This is why I have extended my protection to him.[8] Abul-'Āṣ[ra] was the leader of this caravan therefore please kindly return their possessions."	

A NOBLE FAMILY!

Using the name bank below, find the missing names on the family tree.

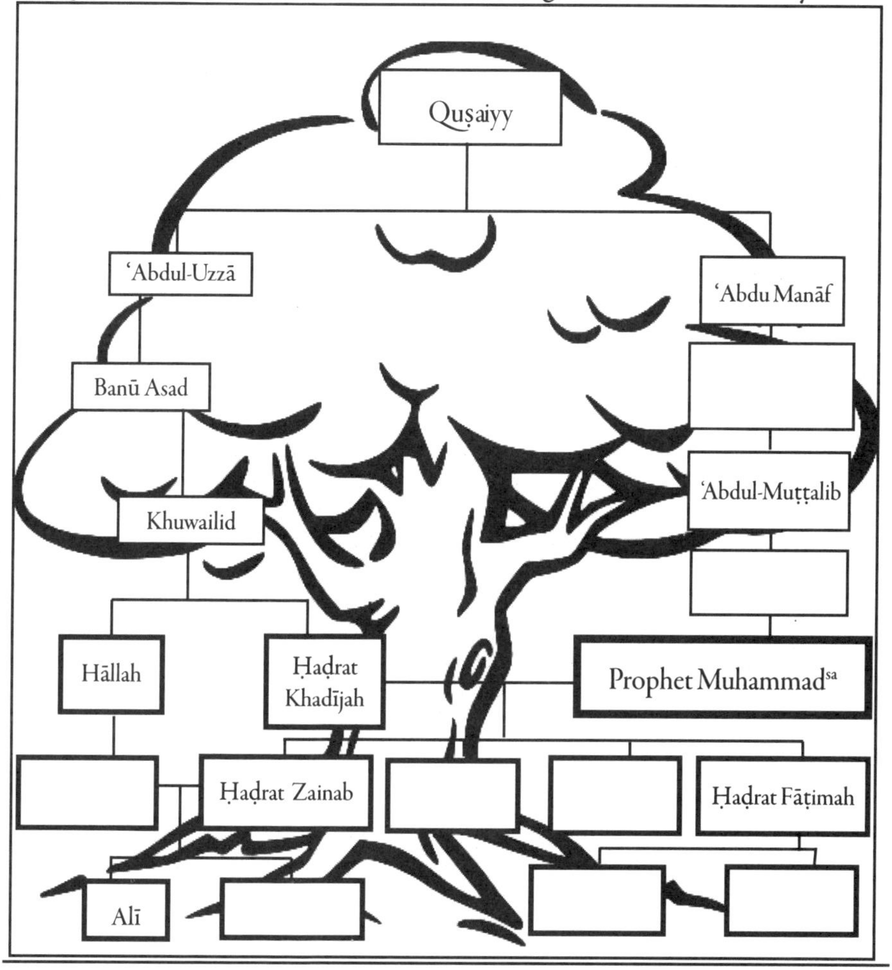

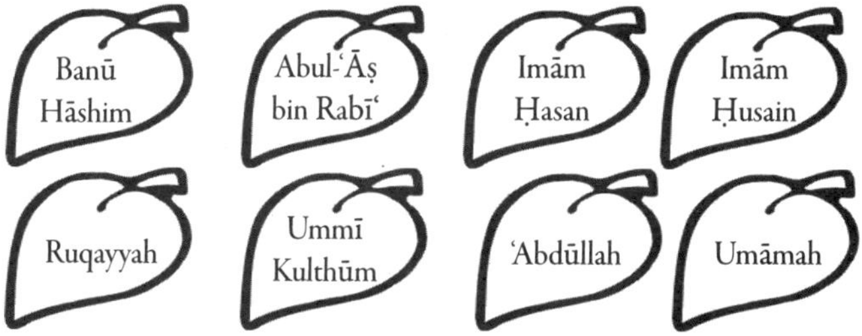

WORDSEARCH

W	T	P	M	T	P	C	A	P	T	I	V	E	B	H	R	R	G	X	P
X	I	T	E	O	H	S	T	P	P	X	A	S	D	O	M	E	C	R	R
M	O	S	X	R	H	A	O	C	F	Y	M	O	V	N	G	L	A	D	O
P	A	Q	D	W	S	F	D	N	Y	U	V	X	Q	O	V	A	R	Y	T
G	S	D	Z	O	K	E	N	M	J	E	E	V	C	U	D	T	A	U	E
J	X	Z	I	P	M	H	C	E	D	G	B	A	B	R	A	I	V	F	C
W	A	N	A	N	J	C	A	U	C	O	T	T	C	A	U	O	A	L	T
R	D	C	I	I	A	B	F	D	T	K	O	V	L	B	G	N	N	U	I
J	G	H	T	Y	N	H	S	Y	I	I	L	L	T	L	H	S	A	F	O
F	M	A	R	R	I	A	G	E	A	J	O	A	D	E	T	H	T	Z	N
P	L	E	D	G	E	J	B	H	V	N	A	N	C	X	E	I	D	P	L
R	X	S	W	G	I	A	H	C	Q	G	D	H	Z	E	R	P	Q	X	Y
E	E	G	Z	I	D	X	U	R	A	N	S	O	M	D	K	J	D	F	J
A	N	C	E	S	T	O	R	S	Z	P	E	S	T	A	Y	X	K	Y	J
M	U	S	L	I	M	J	T	D	L	M	F	A	R	A	B	I	A	R	H

RELATIONSHIP
KHADIJAH
PLEDGE
HONOURABLE
MADINAH
WISDOM
ZAINAB
ANCESTORS
MARRIAGE
NECKLACE
CARAVAN
PROTECTION
ARABIA
PERSECUTION
RANSOM
MUSLIM
DAUGHTER
CAPTIVE

CIRCLE THE ARTIFACT!

Use the clues below to find the missing artifacts. Circle your answer!

1.) When Ḥaḍrat Zainab was leaving Makkah to go to Madīnah she was attacked. Which weapon permanently injured her?

2.) Due to the attack, she fell. Where did she fall from?

3.) When Ḥaḍrat Abul-'Āṣ[ra] returned to Makkah, before declaring that he had become Muslim, he cleared all his accounts and made sure that he did not owe anyone....

4.) The Holy Prophet[sa] received a precious gift which he decided to give to the person most dear to him, his granddaughter Umāmah[ra]. What was the gift?

STUDY QUESTIONS

1.) The Holy Quran:

"And one of His signs is this, that He has created wives for you from among yourselves that you may find peace of mind in them, and He has put love and tenderness between you. In that surely are Signs for a people who reflect."

(Ar-Rūm 30:22)

How do we know that Ḥaḍrat Zainab[ra] and Ḥaḍrat 'Abul-Āṣ[ra] loved each other very much?____________________

____

____

What was the only reason that they were separated from each other?________________________________

____

____

Explain what we can learn from their relationship. ________

____

Think of three reasons why it is important for a husband and wife to love each other.

1____

2____

3____

What is a martyr?____________________________

____

____

Why was Ḥaḍrat Zainab[ra] considered a martyr? __________

____

____

Explain how the body of Ḥaḍrat Zainab[ra] was prepared for her funeral.________________________________

____

How do we know that the Holy Prophet[sa] was grief stricken at the death of his eldest daughter?__________________

____

Find out the different steps which take place in Islamic funerals today and why these particular things happen.

REFERENCES

[1] Azwāj-e-Muṭahharāt wa Ṣaḥābiyāt Encyclopedia, Dr. Dhul-Fiqār Kāẓim, p. 243, Published by Baitul-'Ulūm, Lahore

[2] Azwāj-e-Muṭahharāt wa Ṣaḥābiyāt Encyclopedia, Dr. Dhul-Fiqār Kāẓim, pp. 245-246, Published by Baitul-'Ulūm, Lahore

[3] AAzwāj-e-Muṭahharāt wa Ṣaḥābiyāt Encyclopedia, Dr. Dhul-Fiqār Kāẓim, p. 247, Published by Baitul-'Ulūm, Lahore

[4] Azwāj-e-Muṭahharāt wa Ṣaḥābiyāt Encyclopedia, Dr. Dhul-Fiqār Kāẓim, p. 247, Published by Baitul-'Ulūm, Lahore

[5] Azwāj-e-Muṭahharāt wa Ṣaḥābiyāt Encyclopedia, Dr. Dhul-Fiqār Kāẓim, pp. 247-248, Published by Baitul-'Ulūm, Lahore

[6] Azwāj-e-Muṭahharāt wa Ṣaḥābiyāt Encyclopedia, Dr. Dhul-Fiqār Kāẓim, pp. 249-250, Published by Baitul-'Ulūm, Lahore

[7] (A) Azwāj-e-Muṭahharāt wa Ṣaḥābiyāt Encyclopedia, Dr. Dhul-Fiqār Kāẓim, pp. 250-251, Published by Baitul-'Ulūm, Lahore
(B)Azwāj-e-Muṭahharāt wa Ṣaḥābiyāt Encyclopedia, Dr. Dhul-Fiqār Kāẓim, p. 252, Published by Baitul-'Ulūm, Lahore

[8] Azwāj-e-Muṭahharāt wa Ṣaḥābiyāt Encyclopedia, Dr. Dhul-Fiqār Kāẓim, p. 253, Published by Baitul-'Ulūm, Lahore

[9] Azwāj-e-Muṭahharāt wa Ṣaḥābiyāt Encyclopedia, Dr. Dhul-Fiqār Kāẓim, pp. 253-254, Published by Baitul-'Ulūm, Lahore

[10] Azwāj-e-Muṭahharāt wa Ṣaḥābiyāt Encyclopedia, Dr. Dhul-Fiqār Kāẓim, p. 254, Published by Baitul-'Ulūm, Lahore

[11] Azwāj-e-Muṭahharāt wa Ṣaḥābiyāt Encyclopedia, Dr. Dhul-Fiqār Kāẓim, p. 256, Published by Baitul-'Ulūm, Lahore

[12] Azwāj-e-Muṭahharāt wa Ṣaḥābiyāt Encyclopedia, Dr. Dhul-Fiqār Kāẓim, pp. 255-256, Published by Baitul-'Ulūm, Lahore